PrayerStarters

For
Busy People

Text © 1999 by Daniel Grippo
Published by One Caring Place
Abbey Press
St. Meinrad, Indiana 47577

Library of Congress Catalog Number
99-72386

ISBN 0-87029-328-1

Printed in the United States of America

PrayerStarters

For
Busy People

by Daniel Grippo

A ONE
CARING
PLACE

Abbey Press

Introduction

—— ✑ ——

"Now as they went on their way, he entered a certain village, where a woman named Martha welcomed him into her home. She had a sister named Mary, who sat at the Lord's feet and listened to what he was saying.

"But Martha was distracted by her many tasks; so she came to him and asked, 'Lord, do you not care that my sister has left me to do all the work by myself? Tell her then to help me.' But the Lord answered her, 'Martha, Martha, you are worried and distracted by many things; there is need of only one thing. Mary has chosen the better part, which will not be taken away from her.'"

—Luke 10:38-42.

Through this book, it is hoped that all readers (women and men alike) can learn to be a little bit more like Mary, a bit less like Martha. For indeed, we can all learn much about being attentive to God in our busy lives. The good news is that daily life presents many opportunities for prayer that don't have to be forced and don't have to be planned in advance. All that is required is a little imagination and a willingness to look at everyday situations in a new light.

Many of the reflections are arranged to carry you through a typical day, from early morning to late at night. The remaining reflections cover other "prayable moments" that occur for most of us in the course of a week or a month. The purpose throughout is to demonstrate that in the busiest of days, there are actually numerous opportunities for prayer just waiting to be enjoyed.

Let us begin, then, on the journey all busy people need to make, learning to be a bit less like Martha, a bit more like Mary.

Time-Out!

"How do I pray? I breathe!"
—Thomas Merton

You're busy...stressed...overworked. You don't have time to catch up with yourself, much less with God. How could you possibly hope to find time to pray?

Sometimes you just have to stop whatever you're doing. Call a time-out. Catch your breath. Catch up with your spirit. (The words *breath* and *spirit* come from the same root—no wonder you need to catch both of them right now!)

PrayerStarters

When life is out of balance and you're feeling kind of crazy, let these two words be your prayer—TIME OUT! Call a time out whenever you're:

Tense   Overworked
Irritable   Under pressure
Moody   Testy
Exhausted

Once you declare a time out, you can share your situation with God. Here's a start:

Dear God, I'm so busy I feel out of control. Help me regain my balance and find my center.

"Gimme Five," Says God

"Make everyday life your prayer."
—Karl Rahner, *On Prayer*

How do you spend the first five minutes of your day? Here, in this moment between sleep and wakefulness, is your first prayer opportunity. Before rising to engage the day, you have the opportunity to pause and bring to mind your relationship with God.

You may awake refreshed or groggy, feeling eager and hopeful or fearful and worried about the day ahead. Whatever your condition, let that be the starting point of your prayer this morning.

PrayerStarters

As you prepare to rise, take a moment to praise the Creator. Ask for strength and courage if you feel weak and fearful. Give thanks for your energy if you feel strong. Weak or strong, call to mind the fact that you belong to God.

Before rising, ask yourself what hopes you have for the day. Bring these hopes to God's attention, asking for whatever is required to help you through the day.

Shower With Blessings!

"I used to write 'Prayer' on my calendar, as a reminder to pray regularly. But before long it became so much of a 'technical obligation' for me that I gave up. Now I write 'God' on my calendar."

—unnamed author quoted in *A Man's Guide to Prayer* by Linus Mundy

The morning ritual of bathing is also a time when we begin to plan our day. We think about what's on the calendar and try to figure out how to get it all done. In the midst of it all, how are we to find time for prayer?

PrayerStarters

Many of us use a hot shower as a way to jump-start the day. Let your shower also jump-start your prayers. Take a moment in the midst of your shower to give thanks for the many blessings showered upon you. Let your prayers rise like steam from a hot shower!

Dear God,
    As I begin this new day, I give thanks for your many blessings. Please help me be of service today.

Break the Fast

*"The act of putting into your mouth
what the earth has grown is perhaps your
most direct interaction with the earth."*
—Frances Moore Lappé

Our need for food is persistent. We can't go more than a few waking hours without being reminded of this need by our hunger. Yet there is another kind of hunger, a hunger in our souls. Souls, too, need nourishment. Body and soul, we hunger.

Hunger reminds us of our physical dependence on one another (who among us could bring food to the table without assistance?) and our spiritual dependence on a power greater than ourselves to sustain and nurture us. Food for thought!

PrayerStarters

How will you break your fast this morning? A bowl of cereal? A muffin with jam? Anyone for coffee? As you take that first bite or sip, think for a moment how God nourishes you, in mind, body, and spirit.

Do something to help alleviate world hunger today. Write a letter, make a call, send in a donation, drop off some canned goods. Let that be your way of praying for a world without hunger.

Have You Heard the (Good) News?

*"As cold waters to a thirsty soul,
so is good news from a far country."*
—Proverbs 25:25.

Many of us get our first news of the day in the morning, whether by newspaper, television, radio, internet—or all of the above! As you listen to the news of the world—so much of it bad news, sadly—take a moment to reflect on the Good News that Jesus brought. How different is his message from the one we usually hear. How important it is to make room for the Good News amid the strife and division of our world.

PrayerStarters

Pray the headlines. Pray for the healing of divisions, for peace in place of violence, for honesty and integrity in the face of corruption, for justice everywhere.

Feeling overwhelmed by the bad news? It's okay to "turn the world off" for a while and concentrate on the Good News all around you—in nature, in loved ones, within your own spirit.

Think of one way you can bring Good News to someone today. Let that be your prayer for the day.

The Work of
Human Hands

Laborare est orare.
To work is to pray.
—Benedictine motto

———————— ✿ ————————

When we work at something—a job, a hobby, a household chore—we're engaged in a process of transformation. We're taking one thing and changing it into something new. Although the fruits of our labor are not always immediately visible, our hope is that we have made some improvement along the way.

Transformation is God's own work. We imitate God when we work. We become co-creators, collaborators, associates in the good work of creation.

PrayerStarters

As you pick up your tasks for the day—whether at home, in an office, in a school—think of the ways in which you honor God through your work. Realize that your work is a form of prayer.

As you face the day's challenges, if you feel over-whelmed, let this be your prayer:

Dear God,
Help me to transform problems into possibilities. Help me to see my own role, however humble, as being essential to the unfolding of creation today.

Rest With Me Awhile

"Come to me, all you that are weary and are carrying heavy burdens, and I will give you rest."
—Matthew 11:28

It is important to keep work in balance. Laboring without rest is not good. Moments of refreshment also need to be part of the work day.

Not only does rest refresh, it is also essential to creativity. Some of our most original ideas come to us while we're daydreaming. Leave time in your day for some dreaming!

PrayerStarters

Take a moment to pause from your labors. Enjoy a cup of your favorite beverage, look out the window, take a few deep breaths. As you exhale, whisper a word of thanks to the Creator for giving you energy and life and work to be about.

If you are physically unable to break away from your labors, think of a favorite vacation spot. Go there in your mind until you feel a smile on your face. Let that smile be your prayer this morning.

Reach for the Heavens
at High Noon

Beauty is before me.
And beauty is behind me.
Above and below me hovers the beautiful.
I am surrounded by it.
I am immersed in it....
The beautiful trail.
—Navajo prayer

High noon is the moment when the sun reaches its zenith in the sky, the moment when the day is full. As you become aware of the fullness of the day, become aware of the fullness and beauty of God's creation all around you. Think about what brings fullness to your own life.

PrayerStarters

Go for a noon-time walk today. Drink in the beauty and variety of creation in the fullness of the day. Ponder your wishes and dreams. Where do you find your greatest fulfillment? When and where is your day full, complete, at its zenith?

God encourages your highest aspirations. May you, too, reach your zenith!

Dear God,
Help me to know, and to fulfill, your highest aspirations for me.
Help me to lead a full and fulfilling life.

God—Let's Do Lunch!

Though I am always in haste, I am never in a hurry.
—John Wesley

In many cultures, the noon meal is the main meal of the day. Such a meal, with its several courses, functions to slow the day down—a respite between rounds, a pause, a retreat, a time to collect your thoughts.

Imitate the tradition. Take a little extra time with the noon meal today. Don't rush through it. The more rushed you feel, the more you need time to slow down. Is there a way to be busy without feeling hurried?

PrayerStarters

As you enjoy each course of a full meal—beverage, appetizer, soup, salad, entrée, dessert—say a short prayer of thanks within yourself. Thank God for the many ways in which you are nourished by the fruits of the earth.

If you're feeling isolated, or spend a lot of time working alone or at home, plan a lunch out with a friend. Use the time to share with each other what's going on in your lives. Let this sharing be your prayer today.

Afternoon Delight

Laughter is the beginning of prayer.
—Reinhold Niebuhr

A busy afternoon can wear down the body and the spirit, cause us to feel stressed and disoriented. That's why it's important to make sure every afternoon has a moment of delight.

When we laugh, we release stress and worry, and we connect with one another. We affirm our belief that life is indeed good, despite its burdens and imperfections. Indeed, a laugh is a profound statement of faith and hope!

PrayerStarters

This afternoon, take time for a laugh, a shared joke with a friend or coworker, a phone call to a friend or relative.

Find a way to bring a smile to someone's face this afternoon. Surprise that person with a kind word or gesture, a thoughtful act, a small gift, a witty phrase.

Let humor and a generous spirit be your prayers this afternoon.

Live in the Moment

To...hold infinity in the palm of your hand
and eternity in an hour.
—William Blake

Deadlines loom, the pressure is on. What to do? If we only had more time...

The truth is, we have all the time there is. There's no way to create more of it, so the question becomes: How will we best utilize the time we have?

Spiritual leaders through the ages have taught that the best approach is to practice living fully in the present moment.

PrayerStarters

When you're feeling most rushed on a busy afternoon, take three minutes for yourself. Close the door, take the phone off the hook, and empty your mind of all distractions. Repeat to yourself: I have all the time there is!

Now, practice living in the moment. Allow yourself to be absorbed by the task at hand—that can be your prayer today. Stay rooted in the present and the future will take care of itself.

Commuting With God

"Learn how to pray in the streets or in the country....
waiting for a bus or riding in a train."
—Thomas Merton

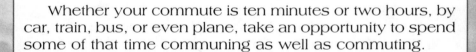

Whether your commute is ten minutes or two hours, by car, train, bus, or even plane, take an opportunity to spend some of that time communing as well as commuting.

What does it mean to commune with God? It involves quieting down, listening for the silence behind the many sounds that surround you, searching for the quiet voice of God in your heart.

PrayerStarters

Try reserving just five minutes of each commute for prayer, for "communing while you commute." If you work at home, take a five-minute "communing walk" when your day is ended.

Use a favorite prayer from your faith tradition, or a prayer you've written yourself. Talk with God about what's going on in your life, or listen for God's quiet voice behind all the sound and motion of rush hour.

Just being aware that you are in God's presence is prayer enough.

A Spirited Workout

*"I wish to preach, not the doctrine of ignoble ease,
but the doctrine of the strenuous life."*
—Theodore Roosevelt

Do you make time in your day for exercise? A jog or brisk walk, a trip to the health club or neighborhood pool, a good game of tennis or a bike ride—physical activity of whatever kind is a great stress buster, especially important for busy folks. Exercise can renew and restore energy, maintain good health, and reduce stress.

The words *health* and *heal* come from the same root, meaning "to make whole." Use exercise to help make your day whole—and holy.

PrayerStarters

Joggers and walkers often use a mantra—a word or brief phrase, repeated over and over—as a form of prayer. It can be a phrase as simple as "God is Love" or "Lord, have mercy." Find a word or phrase that works for you and try it out for a couple of weeks.

Turn a problem over to God during your workout. Ask God to help the two of you work it out together.

Ponder God's strength as you exercise. Think of your workout as a way of building and storing strength for times of adversity.

Messages From God

"And none will hear the postman's knock
Without a quickening of the heart."
—W. H. Auden

What's in the mail today? As we prepare to get the mail, there is a moment of anticipation, of hope. Good news, perhaps? A note from a good friend or relative? A check we've been waiting for? An interesting magazine?

There may also be anxiety mixed in—especially in times of financial distress or illness. Is that bill from the hospital going to arrive today? What will I do if it does?

Above all, the mailbox represents possibility—a place where God is likely to be found.

PrayerStarters

As you prepare to pick up the day's mail (at the mailbox or online), focus on the feelings you are experiencing. These feelings are your prayer at this moment: hope, anxiety, curiosity, anticipation—all are possible. And possibility is what God is all about.

As you reach for your mail, raise your hopes and fears to the God of possibility. Remember, God "knows what you need before you ask...." (Matthew 6:8)

Kitchen Prayer

"Do you want to pray? Slow down!
Eat your peas one by one."
—Ed Hayes, *Pray All Ways*

———————— 🌿 ————————

The kitchen is the place where meals are made, aromas created, warmth generated. It is a place where we generate fuel for our bodies, but also a place that can feed the soul.

When you find yourself preparing a meal, consider the ways in which you are imitating God by doing so. You are nourishing others, as God nourishes you. Take time to "relish" your special role!

PrayerStarters

Savor the aromas that fill your kitchen as you cook. Examine the ingredients you are using to make something that hasn't existed before. As you create something new, you are engaging in God's handiwork.

By participating in the act of cooking, you are doing God's work. You are nurturing life. There could be no higher calling.

Ponder the image of God as a cook—fixing a meal to nourish loved ones.

Chanting Through Chores

To sing is to pray twice.
—St. Augustine

Many evenings, no sooner is the meal done than chores begin. There are plates to wash, dry, and put away; trash to take out; laundry to be done. Kids have homework, adults have yard work or unfinished business from the office. There's always that pesky home repair waiting to be done, too.

Is the busy day never over? Is there a way to make the burden lighter? Is there a way to drive away weariness? There is—it's called song!

PrayerStarters

While doing chores, try using a chant or a simple, repetitive song to drive away weariness and fill the moment with awareness of the divine.

Humming, whistling, and singing have been used for ages to help people get through tedious chores. Use a prayer or church song learned while young. Let your vocal chords do the praying for you, or enjoy a favorite tune on the radio or stereo as you finish the day's work.

Divine Dessert

"L' chaim! *To Life!*"
—Jewish Toast

Why do we love dessert? It's not really a question of hunger—the main meal can generally satisfy that, and an extra piece of bread would serve as well as anything if dessert were really about hunger. No, dessert moves beyond hunger into celebration.

Dessert is that moment in the day when we say, Enough! The work is done, the daily quota has been met—now let us celebrate the goodness and abundance of life. So lift your dessert fork with a prayer—*To Life!*

PrayerStarters

Give yourself a treat tonight, for having finished a day's labors. Take delight in your dessert, whether you choose to reward yourself with a bowl of ice cream, a home-made cookie, popcorn, a piece of candy, or a low-fat substitute for any of the above. It's the idea that counts. You deserve a little reward, and your "just desserts" can also be a prayer of thanksgiving.

Dear God,
   As we reward ourselves for finishing our day's work, we thank you for the work accomplished, the lessons learned, the sweet love shared.

Playfulness
Is Next to Godliness

"The bow cannot always stand bent, nor can human frailty subsist without some lawful recreation."
—Miguel de Cervantes

———————— ✿ ————————

Play is just for kids, right? Nothing could be further from the truth. Sadly, though, nothing could be further from many people's daily routine than playtime.

Play is actually one of the highest forms of human activity, a spontaneous celebration of the goodness of creation. The laughter and joy that healthy play bring are treasures beyond purchase, yet freely offered to all.

PrayerStarters

Take a whole hour today just to play.

If you have children, consider the time you spend playing together as a form of prayer. Spontaneous, laugh-filled, fun-loving—these are qualities that delight God.

Adults can play, too. All they need is a little prodding to bring out the kid in them. Invite some friends over, pull out a board game, a deck of cards, a frisbee, and have some fun. You'll not find a more refreshing form of prayer!

And Now, a Message From Our Sponsor

"Prayer...means listening, pausing, sitting still and simply being for the Lord."
—George Auger, C.S.V., *Living Prayer*

When the work is done, even the busiest folks need a few minutes to put their feet up and relax before bed. Many choose a few minutes of television as a way to unwind. But the constant barrage of commercials can be wearying.

Is there a way to enjoy television without having your senses assaulted? Is there a way to work in a bit of peace and quiet?

PrayerStarters

Next time you're watching television, try hitting the mute button on your remote during commercials. Use the break to rest quietly for a moment in the silence, reminded of the divine whisper that is always being spoken behind the noise.

If you're watching with kids, ask them to figure out, without the sound, the message and values being conveyed by commercials. In a fun way, you can help children be more critical of commercial messages—good practice for a life of prayerful discernment.

Take Five—To Examine Your Conscience

*"You have made us for yourself,
And our hearts are restless until they rest in you."*
—St. Augustine

Just as you can start the day by giving five minutes to God, you can end the day by "taking five" to center yourself.

This "examination of conscience" is a central part of the spirituality of the Jesuit tradition. You can make it a part of your spirituality, too. It can help you rest more easily, peaceful in the awareness of God's love for you.

PrayerStarters

Use the five minutes before sleep to reflect on your day—the highlights and the low points. What can you learn from mistakes made? Invite God to move into the gap and heal the breach, if any exists.

Dear God, As I look back on the day, I feel:
_____.

One thing that happened today that I regret:
_____.

One thing that happened today that I celebrate:
_____.

One thing I will try to do better tomorrow:
_____.

Sabbath Prayers

"Remember the sabbath day, and keep it holy."
—Exodus 20:8

Everyone needs a sabbath—a quiet time away from the business and busy-ness of the week. Most of society used to go along with this notion. Stores and other commercial enterprises closed, and sports games, business conventions, and other events weren't scheduled on Sundays (or, at least, on Sunday mornings).

Not so anymore. No wonder we feel busier and busier. Social expectations have us on the move 24 hours a day, seven days a week.

PrayerStarters

Take a lesson from the biblical writers, Jews and Christians alike, who saw the wisdom in keeping a sabbath. With the agreement of your loved ones, create your own time apart and find ways to spend that time quietly, together.

The sabbath doesn't require constant, intense prayer. Rather, it is a day on which all we do—and especially all we *don't* do—becomes a prayer, because it is devoted to the restoration of our spirits and the recollection of God's many blessings.

Make Time for Worship

"Half an hour's meditation is essential,
except when you are very busy.
Then a full hour is needed."
—St. Francis de Sales

Frazzled at the end of a busy week, you may feel that the last thing you need is to make time for formal worship. Yet, one of the unheralded benefits of worship is that it provides time for sitting quietly, meditating on a reading, singing a hymn, feeling a part of a community—activities that knit our raveled spirits together again.

PrayerStarters

Let worship time be the still point in your turning world this week. Let the prayers and songs of the service wash over you. Sense the rhythm and beauty of the ancient texts. Rest in the sights, sounds, and smells that surround you.

If you are not an active member of a faith community, visit several in your area over the next few months. When one holds promise, return a few more times, talk to members and staff, see if this is a place you can call home.

Pet Prayers

"Pet a furry friend. You will give and get the gift of now."
— Linus Mundy, *Slow Down Therapy*

Many a household contains a wild creature or two—in addition to any children! Furry friends can bring hours of companionship and comfort.

As you feed your pets, notice their trusting dependence on you. Is there a lesson here about our own relationship with God? As you provide the affection, care, and nourishment your pets need, keep in mind that your Creator is doing the same for you—without requiring that you wear a leash!

PrayerStarters

Spend time with a pet today—your own or a friend's—playing, petting, feeding, snuggling. Make of the time you spend together a form of prayer. In your care and feeding of a pet, you mirror and express God's care. In their loyalty and steadfast love, pets model a form of prayer worthy of imitation.

On Hold With God

*"Be patient, therefore, beloved,
until the coming of the Lord."*
—James 5:7

It seems the faster our world gets, the more time we have to spend on hold. Nothing can be as stress-inducing as wading through a pre-recorded, automated answering system, only to be left in telephone limbo...with nothing to do but wait.

Frustrating as it can be, however, waiting on the phone can remind us of the challenges involved in waiting on God in times of uncertainty, fear, or illness. Being on hold can become an opportunity for prayer.

PrayerStarters

Consider being put on hold as a "dry run." By dwelling on the thought of God's trustworthiness, see if you can meditate your way into a peaceful feeling. If so, you have begun to master a skill that is vital in our overstuffed, busy lifestyles—patience!

If you find yourself short tempered, it's a sign that it's time to slow down. Here's one way to start:

"Count your blessings—one at a time and slowly."
—Linus Mundy, *Slow Down Therapy*

Treasured Moments

"The cost of a thing is the amount of what I will call life which is required to be exchanged for it, immediately or in the long run."
—Henry David Thoreau

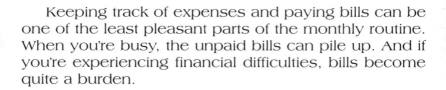

Keeping track of expenses and paying bills can be one of the least pleasant parts of the monthly routine. When you're busy, the unpaid bills can pile up. And if you're experiencing financial difficulties, bills become quite a burden.

Good can come of it all, however. Use your bill-paying and checkbook reconciliation time as an opportunity to examine your priorities. Nothing reveals where our hearts are more vividly than an examination of where our "treasure" goes.

PrayerStarters

Let the checks you write be prayers as well as payments. As you sign each one and place it in an envelope, say a brief prayer concerning whatever financial concerns you have.

When making charitable donations, realize that each donation, no matter how large or small, represents a prayer of its own—expressing hope that the world can indeed be a better place, and indicating your willingness to be a part of that effort.

Traveling Prayers

"Strong and content I travel the open road."
—Walt Whitman

Do you travel for either business or pleasure? Many of us do from time to time. Some people travel constantly. Travel is a two-edged sword—it can be exciting and enriching, but it can also be draining and unsettling.

As you find yourself away from home and loved ones, and missing the support and comforts you're accustomed to, anxiety can arise. And then there's the crowded airports and busy, unfamiliar roads to contend with. Where can peace be found on the road?

PrayerStarters

When traveling, let both your sense of adventure and your discomforts be your prayers. God's steady presence can be a great source of comfort in an environment where everything else is different.

- Think of each trip as a sort of pilgrimage, a journey of faith.

- While away, reflect on the meaning and blessings of home.

- When traveling, pray for a spirit of adventure and an openness to the new.

- Respect and celebrate the diversity of peoples and cultures you encounter.

The Discerning Shopper

*"In an age robbed of religious symbols,
going to the shops replaces going to the church. "*
—Stephen Bayley

Shopping consumes our time and our resources. Responsible shopping also requires discernment— careful examination and tough choices. Even where finances are not a major problem, the hard question of what it means to be a responsible steward of the wealth entrusted to us remains to be worked out, one decision at a time.

As you discern what is best for your home, you are engaging in a form of prayer. You pray for assistance in times of hardship, and you pray for wisdom in times of wealth.

PrayerStarters

A Shopper's Prayer:

Lord, help me distinguish between needs and wants. Help me to honor others' needs at least as much as I honor my own wants. And help me make the sometimes difficult choices that come with being a responsible consumer.

Help me to remember those less fortunate, and to be part of creating a more just social order, where no one has to go without the basic necessities of life. Amen.

Lining Up Priorities

"They also serve who only stand and wait."
—John Milton

Waiting in line is a part of a busy person's life—in fact, there seems to be some unspoken rule of physics that says the faster you need to be on your way, the slower the line in front of you moves!

What's to be done? Consider this "down time" to be "up time"—as you let your spirit rise up to God in prayer. As you wait to be served, God is waiting to be of service to you.

PrayerStarters

While waiting in line, take the opportunity to think about your priorities in life. What should be first in line for you right now? Second? Third?

As you wait to be served, consider what it means to be poor. Poor people spend much of their time waiting in line for basic services—food, medicine, housing, education—that we who are more fortunate often take for granted. Let your time in line today be a time of solidarity with less fortunate people everywhere.

Heavenly Music

"If music be the food of love, play on."
—William Shakespeare, *Twelfth Night*

Music, in the right dose (and, those with kids might add, at the right volume!), has healing power. And fortunately, no life is too busy for music because music coexists so gracefully with other activities.

Invisible to the eye, light as air, this magic called music can surround you with comforting, relaxing sound while you go about your daily rounds.

PrayerStarters

Whether you are commuting to work or communing with nature, bring some music along occasionally. Music is prayer in a different language—a language, according to many spiritual writers, that is God's favorite!

Set aside mood music that you can call on when you're feeling particularly overwhelmed, stressed, harried. Allow the music to soothe your spirit and calm your nerves. Let quiet time with soft music be your prayer today.

Pray for Others— And Yourself

More things are wrought by prayer
Than this world dreams of.
—Alfred, Lord Tennyson

As stress builds in a busy day, you can find relief by calling to mind the needs of others. By shifting your focus for even a moment, you can gain perspective. By calling to mind those who are suffering, you can become aware of your own blessings.

If you yourself are hurting today, allow your pain to rise up as a prayer to God for healing comfort.

PrayerStarters

Here are some PrayerStarters to get you thinking about others:

God, I ask you today to be with _____, who is in need of _____.

God, I thank you today for the blessing of having (name/s) _____ in my life. Help me to be a blessing for others.

God, I pray that you be with the many people who are suffering today and have no one to comfort them. Show me how I can help.

Continue to Choose 'The Better Part'

"Pray out of the reality in which you are; be yourself; pray in the way that is given to you to pray."

—John of the Cross

———— 🍃 ————

The good news for busy people is that daily life is full of opportunities for prayer. Formal, spontaneous, memorized, chanted, interior, spoken, sung—whatever your style and the needs of the moment, the day is positively chock-full of prayer opportunities.

Like buried treasure, these opportunities are not always immediately apparent. But you have assurances of the highest order that, "If you seek, you shall find!"

PrayerStarters

Take a look at your daily routine and pinpoint those moments that are repeated often—your routines. Look for ways to "tuck" some prayer into what's already going on. In this way, you're not adding to your list of duties and obligations, but making use of what's already there.

Throughout the day, strive to be a bit more like Mary and a bit less like Martha. Fulfill your obligations, but cherish and preserve moments where you can simply sit quietly at the feet of the Master and absorb the wisdom of the universe.

About the Author

Daniel Grippo is editor for the One Caring Place division of Abbey Press. He lives in Lenexa, Kansas, where he also writes and teaches. He dedicates this book to Goyo.